Games for Rugby Training:
Using touch rugby as the ultimate game-sense coaching tool

By Dan Cottrell

Want to coach rugby and have fun?

Touch rugby is an ideal way to teach many different skills in lots of different ways while your players enjoy the competitive nature of games.

In this book, I will cover all the main variations and how you can introduce them into your training to:

- Improve decision-making
- Develop specific skills
- Enhance teamship and leadership
- Challenge players under pressure
- Work on fitness
- Enjoy playing the game.

Inside you will find...

- How to coach with touch rugby
- The do's and don'ts of playing touch rugby
- How to change the rules to suit what you want
- Over 20 games
- Games finder to choose the right game

What is game-sense?

It's using games to help players learn skills under pressure in decision making situations.

"Touch rugby" is rugby without full contact. But, and this is important to remember, it is still a game with plenty of contact.

About Dan Cottrell

Dan played first class rugby for Bath and Bristol before becoming Director of Rugby at Cranleigh School. He gained his RFU Level 3 during this time as well as being a coach educator and part of the Surrey Schools coaching team.

He left teaching in 2005 to become editor of International Rugby Coach, Better Rugby Coaching and Rugby Coach Weekly, of which he was a co-founder.

Since leaving teaching he has coached Wales Women at 2010 World Cup, Ospreys U16s, Swansea Schools U15s and his son's youth team. He is also a WRU Level 2 referee.

He was technical editor at Rugby World magazine for three years and has produced numerous books and DVDs on rugby coaching.

Please free to get in touch: dan4rugby@yahoo.co.uk

CONTENTS

1. Games in training

1.1 Five reasons to use this book
1. Have fun at training
2. Improve your players' teamwork
3. Improve your players' decision making
4. Put skills under pressure in game-like situations
5. Have a bunch of simple games which are easy to set up and play.

1.2 What you won't find in this book
1. Drills
2. Techniques

This book is all about games. It's also all about skills. Skills are techniques under pressure, which, in this case, are explored during a game of touch rugby.

So, use this book to give your players plenty of opportunities to put their skills to the test.

1.3 What is the difference between touch rugby and other rugby training games
In this book, we will concentrate on games which are continuous and look close to the real game of rugby, except there's no tackling.

But, beware...there's still contact. And in some of the games, quite a lot.

These games will always use a rugby ball (apart from one game), all the passes will have to be backwards and there's a try line to score over. So, we are not going to show you the rules to rugby netball, bulldogs, Aussie rules and so on. All good games, but this is about touch rugby.

1.4 How to use this book

Here are four ways to use this book:

1. Jump straight to the games section and choose a game that takes your fancy.
2. Look at the games finder to choose a game to suit a need (like handling or fitness or rucking).
3. Read up on how to modify games of touch to adapt to your needs.
4. Work your way through from the start.

But most importantly, play the games and be prepared for chaos.

Chaos is good because it will take time for your players to understand and adapt to the rules of the touch game you are playing. Then they will start to make their own decisions.

2. Touch rugby as a game

2.1 The touch rugby continuum

There's a continuum in touch rugby which branches off in two main ways.

First, there's basic touch rugby which leads to learning points for the full contact game.

Second, there's basic touch rugby which leads to learning points for FIT touch rugby.

We can encourage coaches to use both, with clear signposts of where it will lead them.

2.2 FIT touch rugby

FIT touch rugby is the official game of world touch rugby which is played to a defined set of rules. These rules are used for international and domestic touch tournaments.

It's an exciting form of the game, though its specific tactics narrow the applications for skill development for 15-a-side rugby.

The key skill outcomes are:

1. Preserving space.
2. Quick passing once the defence is squeezed.
3. Footwork.
4. Fitness – the defensive line is always running backwards.

Here are the key rules, adapted from the InternationalTouch.org website:

- Pitch is 70m long by 50m wide.
- Teams consist of up to 14 players with a maximum of 6 players on the field at any time.
- Players may interchange from the side of the field as often as they wish.
- Attacking team has 6 attempts or touches before possession changes unless other rules are infringed.
- If the ball is dropped or knocked-on a change of possession occurs and the game starts with a rollball.
- If a player passes the ball forward, it's a penalty.
- If a player passes the ball after being touched, it's a penalty for a late pass.
- A tap on the mark is taken by non-offending team for penalties. Defending teams must retire 10m.
- A touch is any contact between the player with the ball and a defender. It must be minimum force.
- After a touch the player performs a rollball, stepping over or gently rolling the ball between the feet.
- Players cannot perform a rollball until a touch has been made or a penalty results.

- Players must perform the rollball at the mark or a penalty results.
- The attacking player who gets the ball after the rollball is the half, who can either run or pass.
- If the half gets touched a change of possession occurs and the game restarts with a rollball at the mark.
- At the rollball all defenders must retire or move backwards a minimum of 5m.
- Penalties are awarded against defenders who do not retire 5m for rollballs and 10m for taps.
- A touchdown is scored when an attacking player places the ball on or over the scoreline.

3. Ways to use touch rugby

3.1 Touch rugby for warm ups

Touch rugby is an ideal warm up game to activate minds and muscles. It's played at a lower intensity than full tackling but that mustn't hide important warm up outcomes.

Examples

- Touch rugby in a small area.
- One-hand touch games – lots of tackles so keeping the game less dynamic.
- No mistake touch rugby.

3.2 Touch rugby for decision making

Though all competitive games require some form of decision making, touch rugby can be used to paint different scenarios which are related to the full game. This means both attack and defence have to realign and create or take space to win each encounter, without tackling.

Examples

- Drop off touch, where players are removed from the game for a short period of time.
- Overload touch, where one team has more players than the other.
- Ruck numbers touch, where defenders have to come into the touch-ruck, leaving spaces elsewhere.
- Double touch.
- Kicking allowed in the game of touch.

3.3 Touch rugby for isolating skills

By modifying the touch-tackle process, we can change the type of pass, footwork, support, tackle or ruck decision the players will make.

It's important that there are only one or two focuses for any particular game and then all other skills/techniques are put to one side when making coaching points. For example, if it's catch-and-pass that's the focus, running lines and support are not mentioned during the feedback process. Otherwise the messages are mixed up and the players don't know which skills they are concentrating on.

Examples

- Offload touch for handling, evasion and support.
- Three second touch for handling, evasion and support.
- Grab tackle touch for body positions, footwork before contact and offloading.
- Ruck touch for body positions, ball placement and the contact area.

3.4 Touch rugby for conditioning

Movement and running skills as well as fitness can be explored through touch rugby. So, with modifications on numbers, pitch sizes and tackle conditions, players can work towards fatigue or use specific movement skills in isolation.

Examples

- Drop off touch.
- Using larger pitches.
- A try can only be scored if all the players are inside a certain distancc close to the try line.

3.5 Touch rugby for defence

Despite not being able to fully tackle in touch rugby, it is an excellent way of promoting good defensive habits. With certain modifications, you can replicate the need for square defending (that is, running up so the defender cannot be beaten on the inside or outside), line speed, connectivity in the line and communication.

Examples

- Two-handed touch.
- Square-body touch.
- Defence rewards: if the defence can touch the ball carrier before they run or if the defence can make a touch before there's been two passes. In either case, there's a turnover.

4. Run a touch rugby session

4.1 Essentials for touch rugby

1. It's always clearly defined what the rules are and they are refereed strictly.
2. Teams are mixed up over the course of the game.
3. The coaches don't control the players by shouting on instructions. The players are given the space to make the decisions.
4. There are clear success criteria set out before the game and then, as a coach, measured at the end.

4.2 The touch tackle variations

i) What is a touch tackle?

A touch tackle is where the defender makes some form of contact with the ball carrier.

There are four main types of touch tackle:

- ⚬ FIT touch tackle – one hand anywhere on the body.
- ⚬ One hand below the waist.
- ⚬ Two hands anywhere or below the waist.
- ⚬ Two hands on the front or square shoulder touch.

The FIT touch tackle is the easiest to referee, but like all touch tackling, does need the attacker to "play" the game as well and recognise they are touched.

One hand below the waist is a good game on a wide pitch where you want the attackers to attack spaces. It's also good for slower players, so you could have some players designated as "one-handers".

Two-handed touch means the defenders have to work harder to cover the space. If they can't get in front of the ball carrier, they will have to turn their shoulders to reach across. This creates an opportunity for the ball carrier to step and create a one-handed touch only.

The lower down on the body the touch, the more open the game.

The two-handed touch on the front is more like the real game because it forces the defender to get in front of the ball carrier.

If you add in a shoulder contact, then the ball carrier gets more advantages from trying to avoid contact. The defender has to "touch" with a shoulder to make a tackle.

ii) What happens after the tackle

There are a number of variations of playing the ball after the tackle which have a big bearing on the shape of the game. You can also decide where the offside line happens.

In FIT touch rugby, the ball is played from where the touch happens. This is strictly refereed, so sometimes you will see the ball carrier running back to the point they were touched. The offside line is 5m back from the touch, forcing the defenders to be constantly tracking back. This is pretty tiring too.

In other forms of touch, you can choose the play-the-ball rules (see below) and offside lines to suit the outcomes you want.

iii) Play-the-ball rules

Here are some variations of playing the ball after a touch:

⊘ The ball is played through the legs (a rule in FIT touch). The player behind is called the dummy half or just the half. This is very similar to rugby league. The dummy half cannot score, but can run. If they are touched, it's a turnover.

- The ball carrier passes the ball from where they were touched.
- The ball carrier passes the ball within a time limit, so can continue moving forward.
- The ball carrier has to go to ground and either pop or place the ball
- The ball carrier can only use one hand to pass the ball.

iv) Limiting touches

You can limit the number of touches before a turnover. For example, there are three touches and on the fourth touch, the other team receive the ball.

More touches give the attack more opportunities to develop their play and shape the defence. Less touches puts more pressure on the attacking team.

On the last touch, you could allow the attacking team to kick the ball. See the kicking section for more on how to play this aspect of the game.

v) Offside line

There are three main options for the offside line, which is the line where the defenders must be behind before they can take an active part in the game.

1. The offside line is 5m (or 7m) back from the touch.
2. The offside line is the ball.
3. There's no offside line (for games like offload touch).

vi) Additional rules

You can add in a range of rules as the game progresses to change the situations. Here are some examples:

- The passer must follow their pass.
- The receiver must always be running onto the ball.
- No miss passes.
- call the name of the player who you are passing to.
- Flick the ball through the legs immediately after the tackle.
- The ball is not allowed to touch the ground.
- Kicking the ball is allowed.
- You can only score if all the players are in within a certain distance of the try line.

vii) Scoring methods

The simplest scoring system is one point for a try. A try is scored in a variety of ways depending on your constraints.

- Normal try. The ball is touched down as in a real game of rugby, so diving is allowed.
- Hard ground try. The player simply puts their foot over the try line.
- A one-step try. A player can score if they are touched one step away from the try line.

You can also allocate different points to reward different skills, but beware that complicated points systems can cause the game to slow down. Plus, if you are the referee and coach at the same time, it can be hard to keep score and still make the appropriate interventions.

Here are some examples for points

- Certain players score more points.
- More points are scored if there are more consecutive passes before the try.
- More points are scored if there are less touches.

4.3 Do's and don'ts to make it work

i) Do start the game quickly

A good game is a quick game. Quickly define the size of the pitch, split up the teams and set out the rules.

For a quick game, the fewer the rules, the quicker the game.

ii) Don't have large groups

The worst touch rugby is when there are upwards of 10 players a side. There is too much inactivity and lazy play. The best touch rugby engages ALL the players, ALL the time, leaving them tired at the end of a session. So split up into smaller groups when player numbers approach 10-a-side.

iii) Do let the players work out the tactics

Good games of touch are naturally noisy and competitive. The more you talk the less the players do. Your silence gives them space to shout.

Give the players the chance to decide how to win. One good way is to give them a 30 second timeout to work out how they are going to win the next three minutes of play.

iv) Don't make a big thing of mistakes

Unless the mistake is part of the skill you are testing, just let it go. That keeps the flow of the game good. Also, you can let the specific skill mistake go as well. How? If the rule makes the mistake into a turnover, the players will soon want to change their behaviour. They won't need your advice on that.

v) Do smile

You will set the tone with your energy. Enjoy the game. Celebrate the good moments. Let the rules of the game punish the bad.

vi) Don't let the players use "tap kick" restarts

After a tackle or for a game restart, don't have the players touch the ball on their foot (or worse still their knee). It adds nothing to the game. For a restart you could use a proper penalty tap, that is the ball leaves the hands of the ball carrier. However, any sort of tap leads to the defence being given a cue to run forward. Instead, just start with a pass.

vii) Do use the best ball you have

Play with a match-standard ball. You want players to be focusing on the best skills possible without having to deal with dropped passes because the ball is slippery.

However, if you want to practise for wet weather days, then use an over-pumped old ball.

4.4 Kicking in touch rugby

Kicking is not often a feature of touch rugby but can play an important part in decision-making, but for kickers and for counter attack. If a defending team thinks a kick is coming, they may drop players back, which opens up gaps in the front line defence.

Here are some ideas for rules

1. A team is only allowed to kick after a certain amount of touches, or on their last touch.

2. Once kicked, the chasing team are not allowed to compete for the ball, but only if it's in the air.

4. If the ball goes on the ground, the receiving team has three seconds to gather the ball. This encourages the receiving team to have cover in the backfield. It also encourages the kicker to kick to space.

5. If a receiver makes a clean catch, they can advance 10m without being touched.

4.5 The dangers of rollball

After a touch, you can use a rollball to restart the game. That's when the player puts the ball between their legs and the next player picks up the ball.

This works very well for FIT touch rugby where the defence is retreating. However, for more realistic rugby outcomes, it tends to lead to bad habits. First, it doesn't promote a good body position going forward. Second, it creates a static game if the defence isn't going to be 5m back from the tackle line.

My suggestion is NOT to use rollball unless you are playing to FIT rugby rules.

4. The games finder

All the games that follow promote decision making, evasion, handling and support. However, some promote handling, evasion and support more.

You will also find that some have more contact than others.

Levels

> **Easy** means that all players should find it simple to play. The challenge comes from competition with the opposition.

> **Medium** is a more sophisticated game, accessible to all, but might take some time for players to understand and get to grips with the tactics.

> **Hard** is for more experienced players.

Extra emphasis on

Game	difficulty	handling	fitness	evasion	support	defence	contact
Ball placement	Easy						Yes
No mistake touch	Easy			Yes			Yes
Ruck touch (plus variations)	Medium						Yes
Fiji touch (my man)	Medium		Yes	Yes	Yes		
Fiji touch (two ball)	Medium				Yes		
Three second touch	Medium	Yes	Yes	Yes	Yes		Yes
No ball touch	Medium				Yes		
Drop off touch	Medium		Yes	Yes			
Missing defenders	Medium	Yes		Yes			
Grab tackle touch	Medium			Yes		Yes	Yes
Blitz touch	Hard				Yes	Yes	
Joker touch	Hard				Yes		
All team turnaround touch	Hard		Yes				
360 degree touch	Hard			Yes	Yes		
No look touch	Hard			Yes	Yes		
Ball touch	Hard	Yes		Yes			Yes
Double touch	Hard	Yes		Yes	Yes		
Offload touch	Hard	Yes		Yes	Yes		Yes
Square body touch	Hard			Yes		Yes	

Guide to the games

Name

I've used the name I know the game by, but there is no common language for the names.

Level

Easy, medium, hard

Key points

What you should be looking for and the main rules that separate it from other versions of the game.

How it's played

After you have set out the pitch and split into teams, this is how it's played. I've not included some of the obvious stuff. Restart the game from tries, infringements and going into touch based on what makes sense (or is in the rules).

How much contact

Though the games are "touch-tackle", there's still the chance of some contact. With some games, there's quite a lot, with going to ground, or rucking after the tackle.

Worth noting

Thoughts of how the game might pan out.

Variations

There are lots of variations you could add to each game. See some examples here. I've also noted down some specific ones for some of the games.

Also try

Some of the games lead neatly into others. I've noted them.

Ball placement

Level

- Easy

Key points

- Develops ball placement techniques.
- Poor ball placement after a touch leads to a turnover.

How's it played

- Two-handed touch.
- The touched player goes to ground and presents the ball.
- The next attacking player passes the ball away.
- The defence must get onside behind the prone player.
- Turnovers for poor ball placement.
- Play a limit of six tackles before a turnover.

How much contact

- Players falling on the ground, so some.

Worth noting

- Use this work on all the variations of ball placement you have practised. Be very tough on inaccurate placement.

Variations

- Only allow one type of placement.
- The next attacker can pick and go rather than pass the ball.
- The defender who made the touch has to go to ground (or more than one defender). This is because the defence will always have an extra player on their feet.

Also try *ruck touch*

No mistake touch

Level

- Easy

Key points

- You set the criteria for "no mistakes" and call a turnover when a team makes that mistake.
- Develops a specific skill under pressure.

How's it played

- Play normal touch rugby.
- Set out one or more skills which will be under particular scrutiny. If that skill isn't perfectly executed, the ball is turned over to the other team.
- Possible "skills"
  Call for the ball, carry the ball in two hands, run straight (or diagonally up the field), no miss passes, use footwork before the pass, run onto the pass

How much contact

- Depends on the touch-tackle rules used.

Worth noting

- A good game to use straight after a training exercise to help bed down a skill.
- Don't have too many "mistakes", perhaps one new one this week and a skill from last week.

Ruck touch (plus variations)

Level

- Medium

Key points

- Develops one v one rucking techniques.

How's it played

- Two-handed touch.
- Touched player goes to ground and presents the ball.
- The next attacker and one defender who has not made the touch compete for the space over the ball.
- Call out the winner and that team play the ball.
- The offside line is the back foot of the ruck.
- Turnovers for losing the ruck and for illegal entry into the ruck.

How much contact

- High. Players should be wearing gum shields for this game.

Worth noting

- This is a physical game. A 1 v 1 contest over the ball will isolate skills and reward accurate rucking over just "blasting" through.
- Emphasise square entry, stay low and keep the legs pumping.
- Be tough on the laws around the ruck, making sure players arrive square and stay on their feet.

Variations

- The touched ball carrier goes to ground and you shout "tackle". One player from each team goes on their front, facing each other with the tackled player in between. Shout "ruck" and both players ruck over.
- You do or don't allow the defenders to go for the ball to steal it.
- You allow two attackers to ruck, but only one defender.

Fiji touch (my man)

Level

- Medium

Key points

- Each player can only touch tackle their opposite man in the other team.

How's it played

- Best played with one hand touch.
- Each player is nominated a player on the other team as their opposite man. The ball carrier can only be touch tackled by that nominated player.
- Once touched, the ball carrier has to pass within three seconds.
- The offside line is at the touch tackle.

How much contact

- Little.

Worth noting

- This game is chaotic and tiring. Play on a small pitch with few numbers to start with.

Fiji touch (two ball)

Level

- Medium

Key points

- You carry a spare ball. At any time, you throw that ball into the game and that becomes the new ball.
- Develops quick reactions to changing pictures, like a turnover situation or chasing back from a kick.

How's it played

- Normal touch rugby.
- Play with one ball and you carry another.
- At any stage, throw in another ball. This can be to either side and in front or behind them.
- The players play with the new ball. The current ball carrier has to GIVE you the ball, not throw it at you. Until they do, they can't play an active part in the game.

How much contact

- Depends on your touch rules.

Worth noting

- Throwing the ball high makes the players look up above them. The better players will only look up briefly before scanning for opportunities.

Variations

- The ball is left on the ground after the new ball comes into the game. When you shout change again, that ball comes back into play. You have to be wary that play doesn't come back towards that ball, otherwise players may trip over it.

Three second touch

Level

- Medium

Key points

- Once touched, the ball carrier has three seconds to pass, but they can keep running, though they can't score.
- Promotes good support lines and go forward by the ball carrier.

How's it played

- Two-handed touch.
- Once touched, count down from three. If the ball is not passed by the time you've reached one, then it's a turnover.
- Defenders can stand where they like, there's no offside line.

How much contact

- Some – the touch tacklers will start to realise that they can create turnovers by more aggressive touches on the arms and ball to prevent easy offloads.

Worth noting

- The key to the game is the ball carrier's ability to keep going forward but also to anticipate the touch. They can then shape to pass and look for supporting players

Variations

- Reduce the time limit.
- Make passes after the touch only allowed with one hand.
- Allow the defence to grab the ball carrier to prevent thc offload.
- Allow the attacker to go to ground if they don't think they can pass the ball in time.

Also try *grab touch*

No ball touch

Level

- Medium

Key points

- An outstanding game for communication and spatial awareness, where there's no ball in play. Instead an imaginary ball is passed by calling the name of the receiver.

How's it played

- Two-handed touch.
- Start the teams 10m apart. Give one player in one of the teams an imaginary ball.
- That player can run to score a try. But if he's touched, it counts as a tackle.
- To pass the ball, that player must call out the name of a player who's behind him. That player now has the ball.
- The offside line is at the tackle.
- Allow three tackles before a turnover.

How much contact

- A little.

Worth noting

- Quite a challenging game. You will find that players like to carry the imaginary ball. You will also notice how often players stick to the players' names they are most comfortable shouting out.
- You can disallow long miss passes which skip more than two players. However, there's a case for more of these because it shows good heads-up awareness of where the space is.

Drop off touch

Level

Medium

Key points

A fitness and decision making game. When a defender makes a touch, they have to run back to their try line before re-entering the game.

It should open up gaps in the defence.

How's it played

> Play normal touch rugby, with limited touches before a turnover.

> When the ball carrier is touched, they must pass the ball. However, the defender who has made the touch has to run back to their try line before re-entering the game.

How much contact

Minimal.

Worth noting

> This is a tiring game, so can be a real struggle for younger or less experienced players.

Variations

> Give some players different places to run to get back into the game. For example, slower forwards might run off to the side, fast backs to a corner.

> Drop down touch, where the defender or the nearest two defenders have to go down on their chests.

Also try *missing defenders* for more gaps-in-the-defence type games and *all team touch* for fitness

Missing defenders

Level

◉ Medium

Key points

◉ You nominate a player or two players who cannot make a touch.
   They play as normal in attack. You can do this secretly or bib
   them up.

How's it played

◉ Play normal touch rugby, but one or two players aren't allowed
   to make a touch. They can remain in the defensive line, but
   they must not block the ball carrier.

How much contact

◉ Depends on the touch rules.

Worth noting

◉ It will take time for the attack to realise their advantage. Then
   the defence will have to adjust.
◉ Keep rotating the non-tacklers.

Variations

◉ Shot-gun touch – you shout out a defender's name and they
   have to drop to the ground. They can do a press up, sit up or
   chest down and up before re-entering the game or take a knee
   until you release them.
◉ Shot-gun team touch – put players into groups of two or three.
   When you shout out that group name, they drop to the ground.
◉ Full-back touch – one player in each team (on rotation), stands
   on the try line when their team is defending. They cannot move
   forward, but they can move side-to-side. Their touch counts if
   they make a touch before the ball is put down to score a try.

Grab tackle touch

Level

- Medium

Key points

- A good game to improve tackling confidence, but also support play. If the ball carrier is grabbed and held, they have three seconds to pass the ball or it's a turnover.

How it's played

- On a relatively narrow pitch, a tackle is made when the ball carrier is grabbed and held by a defender. The defender cannot touch the ball or prevent a pass. The ball carrier has three seconds to pass the ball.
- There is an offside line at the grab, so defenders must get out of the way of the pass.
- Defenders aren't allowed to swing the ball carrier around by the shirt.

How much contact

- Quite a lot.

Worth noting

- Because the tackler has to be close enough to make a firm grab, it develops good defensive footwork on the part of the defensive team.
- Also, the ball carrier needs to use footwork to avoid being grabbed.
- Finally, the supporting players will find that if they can run onto the pass, they won't be grabbed so easily.

Blitz touch

Level

- Hard

Key points

- If the defence can make a touch before two passes have been made, then they win the ball.
- This promotes good line speed from the defence, similar to a blitz or rush defence.

How it's played

- Play normal touch rugby, but when touched the ball carrier has to go to ground to present the ball. This creates an offside line.
- The next attacker can run or pass. However, if the attacking team don't make two passes before the next touch, it's a turnover.
- There's no limit on the amount of "tackles".

How much contact

- Not much.

Worth noting

- Keep quiet yourself! Let the teams work out how to attack and defend. Give them a 30 second break to work out tactics.

Variations

- You can start with just one pass then move onto three passes eventually, especially on bigger pitches.
- You can forget passes and say that there's a turnover if the players are caught before they are level with the back foot of the previous breakdown.

Joker touch

Level

- Hard

Key points

- One player from each team is nominated as the joker. If they score, their team retains possession. If they get touched in possession, their team lose the ball.
- It creates a decision-making game on how to use the joker.

How's it played

- Play normal touch rugby with limited touches.
- Nominate a team joker for each team.
- The joker has special powers, but there is a yin and yang to their game too. A try by the joker allows the team to retain possession. However, if the joker is touched in possession of the ball, the ball is turned over.
- Rotate the joker every couple of minutes.

How much contact

- Depends on the version of touch.

Worth noting

- Who should be the joker? You can nominate a player, or let the team decide.

Variations

- The joker can score double points for scoring a try.
- If a joker touches a joker in possession, then that ball-carrying joker's powers are lost until the next try is scored.

All team turnaround touch

Level

𝒪 Hard

Key points

𝒪 A good fitness game, a try can only be scored if the whole attacking team is within 10m (say) of the try line PLUS, once a try is scored the defending team has to run back to the halfway before turning to defend.

How's it played

𝒪 Play two-handed touch on a large pitch. A good variation for this game is three-second touch.

𝒪 To score a try, the whole attacking team must be within a certain distance of the try line when the ball is touched down. The ball is turned over if not.

𝒪 Once a try is scored, the attacking team turn around and play in the other direction after a count of 5 (or more depending on the players involved).

𝒪 In the meantime, the defending team can only defend once they have reached the halfway line. Stragglers after the attack has started have to return to the try line.

How much contact

𝒪 Not much.

Worth noting

𝒪 This is extremely tiring and probably suits older players because they will have the mental toughness to keep going.

𝒪 Your refereeing will need lots of energy to keep players "onside". Think of a drill sergeant attitude for this game.

360 degree touch

Level

- Hard

Key points

- Call out which try line each team is attacking, and change that during the game, so players have to realign quickly.
- This develops communication and awareness of where the spaces are.

How's it played

- Use a rectangle shape as a pitch so there's a possible wide pitch or possible narrow pitch.
- Play any variation of touch rugby.
- Start with a try line for each team, and then, as the game progresses, call out a change. It can be mid-play or after an infringement.

How much contact

- Depends on your version of touch.

Worth noting

- It's best to have a reference point for each try line. For example, the clubhouse, the trees, the road or just use coloured cones.
- The easiest version has north-south or east-west as the directions to the try line. If you want to really mess with their minds, try something like north-east. So one team attacks at right angles to the other team's attack. The team in possession can only pass backwards in the direction they are playing.

No look touch

Level

- Hard

Key points

- When the ball carrier is touched, he immediately puts the ball between his legs and throws it behind him. If his team don't catch it, it's a turnover.
- This form of the game works most on the role of support players getting in behind the ball carrier.

How's it played

- Play normal touch rugby.
- When the ball carrier is touched, they have to, without looking, put the ball between their legs and throw it behind them. If the ball touches the ground, it's a turnover.

How much contact

- Not much.

Worth noting

- There's a certain amount of mistakes at the start of this game, but be patient as the players get used to being in support and the skill of popping up the ball behind them.
- This is also good for promoting good body angles as the players have to be square at the contact area and keep the ball away from the opposition.

Ball touch

Level

- ⭕ Hard

Key points

- ⭕ If a defender touches the ball, then it's a turnover.
- ⭕ This works on ball manipulation close to contact and on quick transference of the ball. It also develops good footwork to create space between the defender and the ball carrier.

How's it played

- ⭕ This is a very fluid game. There's no "touch-tackle". The only way of preventing the attacking team scoring is to touch the ball. If this happens, there is a turnover.

How much contact

- ⭕ Quite a lot.

Worth noting

- ⭕ There's quite a lot of contact in this game, with defenders trying to wrap up the ball carrier if they can't actually touch the ball. You can disallow this for a more fluid game.

Double touch

Level

 Hard

Key points

- It's a turnover if the ball carrier gets touch by two separate players. This creates space as defenders are drawn in and promotes good footwork and quick offloading.

How it's played

- The ball carrier can run and pass if they are touched once, but not score. If they are touched another time by a different defender, then it's a turnover.
- Unlimited "one-touches".
- Use two-handed touch.

How much contact

- Some.

Worth noting

- This is quick and tiring game for attacking teams. They have to keep the ball moving to where the defence is most spread.
- Do allow the ball to go on the ground, because you want the players to pass away from trouble and that might mean some high pressure passes.

Offload touch

Level

- Hard

Key points

- Once touched, the player goes to ground and pops up the ball to a team mate OR can only pass with one hand.
- Either version promotes better continuity, ball manipulation and support players reading the movement of the ball carrier.

How it's played

- When the ball carrier is two-handed touched, they have to drop to the ground immediately and pop up the ball within two seconds. The offside line is the ball, so defenders cannot intercept the pass.
- OR, the ball carrier, once touched, has to use a one-handed pass within two seconds (make it longer for less skilled players). Again the offside line is the ball.

How much contact

- Some contact, especially for players rolling on the ground.

Worth noting

- This is a very dynamic game and should get supporting players running onto the pass. If they're not, then penalise players who take the ball standing still.
- Expect mistakes and be encouraging.
- Try it out on wet days to see if the players can adapt their habits.

Variations

- For the pop off the ground, you can make two defenders go on their fronts as well. This is a particular favourite of the All Blacks.

Square body touch

Level

⬭ Hard

Key points

⬭ After the touch, the ball carrier slows to a walk but crouches. A defender gets in front of them and pushes them. The ball carrier goes to ground and the ball is played away.
⬭ With the variations, it develops body positions, realignment and possible contact skills.

How's it played

⬭ Split into three teams. Two teams attack, one defends.
⬭ Play two-handed touch rugby. When the ball carrier is touched, he slows to a walk and crouches down.
⬭ A defender gets in front of the ball carrier and puts a hand on each shoulder, pushing him backwards if they can.
⬭ When you call "tackle", the ball carrier goes to ground and presents the ball. The next support player has to clear away the defender and the next supporter passes the ball away.
⬭ The offside line is at the tackle.

How much contact

⬭ Quite a lot.

Worth noting

⬭ The ball carrier should be in a good body position to go to ground and present the ball dynamically. Emphasise this point.

Variations

⬭ The defender can go for the ball once the attacker goes to ground.
⬭ The defender can be more aggressive in the push.

Disclaimer

The information in this book is meant to supplement, not replace, proper rugby training. Like any sport involving speed, equipment, balance and environmental factors, rugby poses some inherent risk. The author advises readers to take full responsibility for their safety and know their limits. Before practicing the skills described in this book, be sure that you do not take risks beyond your level of experience, aptitude, training, and comfort level.

Printed in Great Britain
by Amazon